# Generis

PUBLISHING

**Dibakar Pal**

## *WOOD-LAND BLOSSOMS*

### *(A collection of creative nonfictions)*

**CIP a Camerei Naționale a Cărții**


**Pal, Dibakar.**

Wood-land blossoms : (A collection of creative nonfictions) / Dibakar Pal. – Chișinău : Generis Publishing (Online Marketing Group), 2020 (Print on demand). – 63 p.

ISBN 978-9975-119-10-8.

821.111(540)

P 14



Cover image: www.pixabay.com

Generis Publishing
Online orders: www.generis-publishing.com
Orders by email: info@generis-publishing.com

*DEDICATION*

*IN MEMORY OF UNRECOGNISED AUTHORS*

# TABLE OF CONTENTS

*OF CELEBRATE*

## ABSTRACT


Celebration revises both the faces and relations. Also it determines the fates. It may close the previous relations simply ignoring and without caring. It may renew a lost relation as well. Also it may open completely a new account of love and life. Festival paves the way to meet each other. Even the orthodox family relaxes the rigidity of vigilance. As such both fiancé and fiancée use this opportunity of being closer without any fail. Here lies the utility and importance of celebration to the uniquely needy persons.

**KEYWORDS:** Celebrate, enjoy, festival, famous, occasion


## INTRODUCTION

Creative writing is based more on manifestation rather than on expression. It does not inform, rather it reveals. So it bears no reference. The best creative writing is critical, and the best critical writing is creative. This article is an outcome of thinking about creative writing meant for a general readership. As such, I have adopted a free style methodology so that everyone can enjoy the pleasure of reading. As you might know, Francis Bacon (1561-1626), the immortal essayist, wrote many essays namely 'Of Love', 'Of Friendship', 'Of Ambition', 'Of Studies', and so on. The multiple-minded genius correctly pointed out that all the words of the dictionary can be used as themes for essays. But little has been done since his death to continue or finish his monumental task. Bacon's unique individual style of presentation ignited my imagination and encouraged me to write creative essays as a method of relieving a wide range of emotions through catharsis.

# ARTICLE

Celebrate is to mark a happy or important day, event, etc. with a social gathering where people can enjoy themselves e.g. celebrate Christmas/somebody's birthday/a wedding anniversary; celebrate a victory/success.

It is to make famous. It is to perform with proper rites and ceremonies, as mass, the Eucharist, marriage, etc. It is to enjoy oneself in some way on such an occasion. For example: It's my birthday – let's celebrate e.g. with alcoholic drink. It is of a priest to lead a religious ceremony e.g. celebrate Mass/ the Eucharist. It is to praise or honour somebody/something e.g. a movie celebrating the life of Abraham Lincoln.

Colloquially, it is to have a good time. It is to engage in festivities, usually after a special event etc. It is widely known. It is to engage in festivities after success etc.

Thus celebrate is to commemorate an anniversary, holiday, etc. with ceremony or festivity. It is to proclaim. It is to praise widely or to present to widespread and favourable  public notice, as through newspapers, novels, etc. It is to solemnize. It is to perform a ritual, ceremony, etc. publicly and formally. It is to mark a happy occasion by engaging in some pleasurable activity.

Celebrated means famous. It is renowned. It is well-known. It is much spoken of. It implies distinguished e.g. a celebrated actor/writer/pianist; a celebrated poet, artist. Further example: Burgundy is celebrated for its fine wines. The names of those martyrs are still celebrated in our songs.

Celebration is the act or an instance of celebrating or an occasion of celebrating. It is that which is done to celebrate anything. It is any solemn ceremony. It is an extolling e.g. birthday celebrations; a day of celebration.

Celebratory is of a celebration. It is marking an important occasion, etc. a celebratory mood/atmosphere; a celebratory dinner/drink/banquet.

Celebrity is a famous or well-known person. It implies fame. It means renown.  It is wide recognition. It is a well-publicized person. It is the condition of being celebrated. It is notoriety. It is a person of distinction or fame. It is a celebrated person e.g. celebrities of stage and screen i.e. well-known actors and film stars. It is being famous. For example: His researches have made him a celebrity.

Celebrant is a priest leading a church service, especially the Eucharist, or a person attending it. It is the officiating priest in the celebration of the Eucharist. It is the principal officiant at a rite. It is a participant in a public religious rite. It is a participant in any celebration. It is a person who praises or extols a person or thing. It is any person who celebrates. It is celebrator.

Celebrate, commemorate, solemnize, observe, keep, honour, laud, glorify are synonymous.

Celebrate means to mark an occasion or event, especially a joyous one, with ceremony or festivity e.g. let's celebrate your promotion.

To commemorate is to honour the memory of some person or event as by a ceremony e.g. to commemorate Lincoln's birthday.

To solemnize is to use a formal, serious ritual e.g. to solemnize a marriage.

Observe and the less formal keep mean to mark respectfully a day or occasion in the prescribed and appropriate manner e.g. to observe, or keep, a religious holiday.

All cannot celebrate. All does not want not to celebrate. A serious person considers celebration as merely wastage of time. By that time he can do other works or earn more. To such a serious person money is sweeter than honey. But always works renders a person bored. To get relief from daily monotonous routine celebration is an easy avenue to revitalize the tensed and tired nerves.

Celebration offers relief to the tired nerves. A revitalized person regains his lost enthusiasm after celebration. The renewed person can again engage himself with full vigor and enthusiasm. So celebration does not waste time due to break rather after recession the total outcome is far better than without break or no break at all. As such recession or interval is observed and is a must in any organization.

Only a jovial person can celebrate. Also celebration depends on luck and temperament as well. He who is satisfied with less can celebrate more. Conversely, he who is satisfied with more can celebrate less. Both these satisfaction and dissatisfaction depend upon personality traits and varies person to person that makes individual difference.

He who hankers after much has to wait till he is happy with much success. Thus he deprives him from early enjoyment through celebration. Since life is only for once. An intelligent person drinks life to the lees whenever he gets chance. But a greedy person deprives himself hankering after mundane gain. In fact enjoyment though is a mundane affair is quite heavenly in nature. A person can attain the essence of divinity through celebration.

Celebration revises both the faces and relations. Also it determines the fates. It may close the previous relations simply ignoring and without caring. It may renew a lost relation as well. Also it may open completely a new account of love and life. Festival paves the way to meet each other. Even the orthodox family relaxes the rigidity of vigilance. As such both fiancé and fiancée use this opportunity of being closer without any fail. Here lies the utility and importance of celebration to the uniquely needy persons.

A poor person celebrates in spite of his poverty. The experienced soul knows that misery is his ever inseparable companion. He is accustomed to stay peacefully with his misery. As such he does not deprive him from celebration. He enjoys all and every kind of celebration thereby remains free form mundane cares and anxieties. He has nothing to lose except poverty and sad luck. The rich is envious of poor person in this respect. Thus property is a hindrance for free and fair enjoyment. And poverty opens the door to welcome enjoyment.

A rich person hankers after money round the clock. He is not happy what he has gained. He is always unhappy what he has gained. Thus he is engaged twenty four hours in thoughts for gaining more. As such he cannot enjoy property what he has already gained.  The paradox is that he is happy with holding instinct only. As such he boasts of his huge property. Simultaneously he is unhappy for not quenching his unlimited thirst.

All cannot be celebrity. It needs talent. It demands temperament. Luck accelerates to achieve it. All are not fortunate. Fortune smiles only at few persons. This answers why we see few celebrities around us.

Celebration depends upon time, place and mood. Also environment is an important factor for its implementation. In bad time a person can't celebrate thereby enjoy due to off mood. A person can enjoy more after finishing his duties and responsibilities.

An intelligent person does not join pleasurable activity always.  To him call his duty is more important than the call of beauty. A beautiful face is enjoyable. That very face is enjoyable more after fulfilling duties. The ingredient of beauty is identical before and after duty. It offers more pleasure when there are no cares and anxieties. That is possible after fulfilling imposed duty and responsibility. As such an intelligent person is engaged after fulfilling his duties.

A good student does not waste time. He does not join all the festivals. He reads first. After that in leisure hours he enjoys. He knows that meaning of student life is to build the career. Later on after completion of career whole life can be used and utilized for celebration. As such the genius uses his every moment of student life very judiciously. This cautious judgment paves the way for future success.

In contrast, an inattentive student always joins all the celebrations. He is an ADIDAS i.e. all day I dream about sports. In this way he wastes his valuable precious time of student life. But, if a single moment of student life is misused then thousand moments of future can hardly compensate that deficiency of student life. Man realizes this misuse of time when he reaches the autumn of life. In that belated period of life he is quite undone except mourning.

It seems unguarded childhood coupled with unshaded infant are liable to be the victim of utter and untimely ruin. Misfortune follows him like the shadow. As such misfortune dogs him wherever he goes. Such a victim suffers till he breadths his last.


## CONCLUSION

Sugar is sweet. To a frustrated person it is not so sweet. But to a successful person it is more than sweet. Love does not exist in vacuum. If a lover ignores duty for the sake of beauty then that very guy will ignore his previous beauty to respond to the call of another better beauty and so on. It is an endless drama. An intelligent fiancée knows it. She inquires and interrogates the guy regarding his past celebrations. Then she takes decision. Here lies the outcome of involvement in celebration.


## REFERENCES

No reference, since the present article is an outcome of Creative Writing

# *OF CERTAIN*

## ABSTRACT

Any event is the outcome or resultant effect of so many known or unknown and uncontrollable factors. As such certain is a very difficult assumption. It may not be exact. It is nearly expected. The term certain is used to counter uncertainty. Everything is uncertain except death which is sure and certain.

**KEYWORDS:** Certain, confident, destined, sure, inevitable, bound, true, unquestionable

## INTRODUCTION

Creative writing is based more on manifestation rather than on expression. It does not inform, rather it reveals. So it bears no reference. The best creative writing is critical, and the best critical writing is creative. This article is an outcome of thinking about creative writing meant for a general readership. As such, I have adopted a free style methodology so that everyone can enjoy the pleasure of reading. As you might know, Francis Bacon (1561-1626), the immortal essayist, wrote many essays namely 'Of Love', 'Of Friendship', 'Of Ambition', 'Of Studies', and so on. The multiple-minded genius correctly pointed out that all the words of the dictionary can be used as themes for essays. But little has been done since his death to continue or finish his monumental task. Bacon's unique individual style of presentation ignited my imagination and encouraged me to write creative essays as a method of relieving a wide range of emotions through catharsis.

## ARTICLE

Certain means free from doubt or reservation. It implies confident. It is destined. It is sure to happen, etc. For example: He is certain to be there. It is inevitable. It is bound to happen. For example: They realized then that war was certain. It is established as true or sure. It is unquestionable e.g., certain evidence. It is certain

"

that he tried. It is agreed upon e.g. on a certain day; for a certain amount; a certain charm. It is that may be depended on. It is trustworthy. For example: His aim was certain. It is some though not much. For example: His smile is tinged with a certain sadness. It is slight. It is little. For example: There was a certain coldness in her attitude towards me.  I felt a certain reluctance to tell her the news. It is steadfast now obsolete. It is surely e.g. to know for certain.

Certain is fixed, settled, or determined. It is not failing. It is reliable. It is dependable e.g. a certain cure. It is controlled. It is unerring e.g. his certain aim. It is assured. It is positive e.g. certain of his innocence. It is appreciable e.g. to a certain extent. It is a certain indefinite number. It is certain ones e.g. swift and certain disaster

Certain is not named or described, though definite and perhaps known. For example: "A certain man went down from Jerusalem to Jericho".

Convinced, satisfied, sure, indubitable, incontestable, irrefutable, determined are synonymous to certain.

Certainly is beyond doubt. It is without doubt. It is surely. It is assuredly. For example: I will certainly be there. It implies yes, of course. For example: Certainly, take the keys. It is surely. It is to be sure. For example: She certainly is stupid.

Certainty is the quality, state, or fact of being certain. It is something certain. It is anything certain. It is definite act. It is an assured fact.

Certainty is slang cert, sometimes in the phrase dead cert.

Moral certainty is moral.

For certain is as assuredly. It is without doubt.

Of a certainty, in archaeology, means without a doubt. It is certainly.

For certain is an idiom means without doubt. For example: I could not say for certain when he will arrive. I did not yet know for certain.

Make certain is to make sure. It is indisputable. It is confident, convinced. It is destined, undoubtedly going, to do.

Make certain that means to find out whether something is definitely so. For example: I think there is a train at6.30 but you ought to make certain.

Make certain of something/of doing something means to do something in order to be sure that something else will happen. For example: You would better leave now if you want to make certain of getting there on time.

Certain of means some particular members of a group of people or things. For example: Certain of those present had had too much to drink.

A lady of a certain age is one no longer young.

In a certain condition is a euphemism for pregnant.

Certainty, certitude, assurance, conviction, truth are synonymous.

Certainty suggests a firm, settled belief or positiveness in the truth of something. Certitude is sometimes distinguished from the preceding as implying an absence of objective proof, hence suggesting unassailable blind faith. Certitude is a certain person implying some degree of contempt. Assurance suggests confidence, but not necessarily positiveness, usually in something that is yet to happen. For example: I have assurance of his continuing support. Conviction suggests a being convinced because of satisfactory reasons or proof and sometimes implies earlier doubt.

Doubt, skepticism are antonym of certainty.

Certain and sure are often used in the same way. For example: Are you sure/certain that you locked the door? They are sure/certain to be late. We must make sure/certain that we arrive on time.

You can say it is certain i.e., not 'it is sure'. It is certain that thousands of people died during the revolution.

Sure can often sound less strong than certain, especially in conversation. For example: I'm sure she will come if she can i.e. I believe/hope she will. I am 100 per cent certain she will come i.e. I have no doubt.

Thus all certain is sure, but all sure may not be certain.

The certain pronounced by an honest person is cent percent assured. The guarantee by a dishonest person is full of doubt. Thus certainty depends upon the source. It is a belief depending upon the past experience. It is a statistical interpretation.

If an honest person fails to keep promise then the cause is certain. In case of failure of a dishonest person it is quite doubtful. If a dishonest person keeps his promise then it is news. It seems that he kept his promise under severe compulsion or he could not escape from the opponent party.

A wise is a versatile genius. A politician is a vacillating genius. He always vacillates to befool the public. He always wants to be certain in his gain. Profit is his only single agenda.

A certain thing is difficult to occur. The earth is moving and for that everything is moving. One thing occurs due to resultant effect. One thing does not happen that is also due to resultant effect. One thing occurs overcoming so many uncontrollable and sometimes unheard, unprecedented parameters even. So, one should not be sure of anything till it happens. One cannot be certain of happening something. One should not give or can't give cent percent guarantee of repeating the previous occurrence.

From an uncertain thing certainty cannot be expected. He who is uncertain does not have the experience of certain. Certainty is just like good will, much valued in love and business as well. It has both qualitative and quantitative value.

Taste of any product may not be certain always in spite of identical recipes. Mood or temperament is not always certain. Emotion always fluctuates. Emotion is uncontrollable since it is influenced by many uncontrollable factors.

Any event is the outcome or resultant effect of so many known or unknown and uncontrollable factors. As such certain is a very difficult assumption. It may not be exact. It is nearly expected. The term certain is used to counter uncertainty.


## CONCLUSION

Everything is uncertain except death which is sure and certain. But the paradox is that occurrence of certain death is quite uncertain. Man is mortal. It is universal truth. Man must die. But the time of death is quite uncertain. A man may die at the age of nine or nineteen or ninety or whatever the age may be in between. As such occurrence of certain death is controlled by uncertainty. Thus certainty is controlled by uncertainty. Similarly, death is uncertain. But occurrence of uncertain death is quite certain. Thus, uncertainty is also controlled by certainty. Here lies the uniqueness of certain in the light of uncertain.

## REFERENCES

No reference, since the present article is an outcome of Creative Writing

# *OF CONVENTION*

## ABSTRACT

Convention is held to make a treaty for world peace. Pages after pages are printed. They say, treaty is not an agreement at all. It is simply a diplomatic farce. Rather it is a strategy of the mightier to kill time and prepare for action against the opponent. The mightier breaks the treaty and the weak opponent has to bear the torture. Here lies the uniqueness of convention.

**KEYWORDS:** Convention, agreement, consent, custom, formal assembly, common purpose

## INTRODUCTION

Creative writing is based more on manifestation rather than on expression. It does not inform, rather it reveals. So it bears no reference. The best creative writing is critical, and the best critical writing is creative. This article is an outcome of thinking about creative writing meant for a general readership. As such, I have adopted a free style methodology so that everyone can enjoy the pleasure of reading. As you might know, Francis Bacon (1561-1626), the immortal essayist, wrote many essays namely 'Of Love', 'Of Friendship', 'Of Ambition', 'Of Studies', and so on. The multiple-minded genius correctly pointed out that all the words of the dictionary can be used as themes for essays. But little has been done since his death to continue or finish his monumental task. Bacon's unique individual style of presentation ignited my imagination and encouraged me to write creative essays as a method of relieving a wide range of emotions through catharsis.

## ARTICLE

Convention is a general agreement, especially agreement on social behavior etc. by implicit consent of the majority. It is a custom or customary practice, especially an artificial or formal one. It is a formal assembly or conference for a common purpose.

In US it is an assembly of the delegates of a political party to select candidates for office. In history it is a meeting of Parliament without a summons from the sovereign. It is a formal agreement. It is an agreement between states, especially one less formal than a treaty.

In Cards it is an accepted method of play, in leading, bidding, etc., used to convey information to a partner. It is the act of convening.

Thus, convention is a conference of members of a profession, political party, etc. e.g. a teachers'/dentists' convention; hold a convention; the US Democratic Party Convention i.e. to elect a candidate for president.

It is what is generally believed or expected about how people should act or behave in certain circumstances e.g. defy convention by wearing outrageous clothes; a slave to convention i.e. somebody who always follows accepted ways of doing things.

It is a way in which something is usually done e.g. the conventions which govern stock-market dealing; diplomatic conventions; a copyright convention.

It is general agreement on the usages and practices of social life e.g. bohemian revolt against convention. It is a customary practice, rule, method, etc. It is an usage e.g. the soliloquy was an Elizabethan dramatic convention.

It is an agreement between states, rulers, etc. that is less formal than a treaty e.g. the Geneva Convention i.e. about the treatment of prisoners of war, etc.

Conventional is depending on or according with convention. It is of a person attentive to social conventions. It is usual. It is of agreed significance. It is not spontaneous or sincere or original. It is of weapons or power and non-nuclear. In art it is following tradition rather than nature.

Conventional, often in derogatory sense, is tending to follow what is done or considered acceptable by society in general e.g. conventional clothes/behavior.

Conventional is following what is traditional or the way that something has been done for a long time e.g. a conventional design/method. It is established by general consent or accepted usage e.g. conventional symbols. It is ordinary e.g. conventional phraseology. It is not natural, original, or spontaneous e.g. conventional behavior.

Conventional, especially of weapons, is not nuclear e.g. conventional missiles/warfare; a conventional power station i.e. using oil or coal as fuel, rather than nuclear power.

The conventional wisdom i.e. the generally accepted view is that high wage rises increase inflation. It is the generally accepted belief with regard to some matter, or the set of beliefs held by most people.

Conventionalism is adherence to or advocacy of conventional attitudes or practices. It is a conventional expression, attitude, etc. As per Philosophy, it is the view that fundamental principles are validated by definition, agreement, or convention.

Conventioneer, in U.S is a delegate or member attending a convention.

Conventionalize implies chiefly Britain conventionalize.

Convention is omnipresent. Man experiences it in its various forms and features in real life.

For example: Convention dictates that a minister should resign in such a situation. By convention the deputy leader is always a woman. She is very conventional in her views.The convention of the parliament/of the annual general meeting is obeyed by the members as faithfully as possible.There is a tendency among the young to flout conventions. Man is a social animal and a stupid slave to social conventions. Conventional outlook/method is declining with the advancement of the civilization.

Lazy and orthodox persons do not like to change the convention. Change has two outcomes either good or bad. As such a cautious person likes not to change the system lest he is held responsible for the changed situation from good to bad or positive to negative. They say, "Everybody's mother is nobody's mother".  As such in public works change may not be good always. But in private case change becomes always good due to strict vigilance round the clock.

Convention originates from what should be best as per ethics more than law. If a convention still serves purpose at present better it is to continue further. If it does not serve the purpose in the changed situation then it should be amended so that it suits and serves the present purposes. But it is a million dollar question who will take the headache for social reformation! The reply is either a patriot or a shrewd rich whose interest will be fulfilled.

Convention is not legal binding but moral obligation. Hospitality is a chief ingredient of a rich culture. Some societies value guest most. To such a society to serve guest is not merely etiquette rather it is more than that. It binds the social relations intimately coupled with close and friendly manner.

In some societies old parents are cared more. It is their conventional culture. The citizens of that society are taught to look after their old parents and relatives sincerely. It is their judicious investment. The little children observe this hospitality and learn it. Then today's youth will be old and inactive in course of time. Then the old persons of future will also get the same return. If a person neglects his old parents then he cannot expect any help from the society rather he will die uncared. Thus he is paid back by his own coin. It comes back as boomerang. It is his own created convention that acts as his own Frankenstein.

Some nations consider old and children as elite class. Such a nation preaches that we are not impartial, rather partial to our old and children. They enjoy the most opportunity of the society. To care old parents means to repay the debt. To care children paves the way to build the nation healthy, wealthy and wise.

Convention has a force of movement. Though it is casual in nature, it can serve the serious matters also. It can influence the treaty. One person of opponent who is tender in nature follows convention and can influence even the hardened soul of the opponent.

Conventionally dressed/designed approach is valued much in an orthodox society. Conservative persons are its sole patron. It has traditional value to the elite class. Royal society maintains it and reminds the glorious past and repents for the by gone days.

There is a great relation between convention and rituals. Rituals are observed as convention. In other words as per convention rituals are followed. Thus convention is the container and law is the content.


## CONCLUSION

Convention is held to make a treaty for world peace. Pages after pages are printed. They say, treaty is not an agreement at all. It is simply a diplomatic farce. Rather it is a strategy of the mightier to kill time and prepare for action against the opponent. The mightier breaks the treaty and the weak opponent has to bear the torture. Here lies the uniqueness of convention.

## REFERENCES

No reference, since the present article is an outcome of Creative Writing

# *OF CONVINCE*

## ABSTRACT

There are two types of persons. The first category is convinced easily. The second category is not convinced easily. The merit of first category is that he is convinced easily. The demerit of first category is that he is convinced easily. Such a dual character is so unique that he possesses both merit and demerit simultaneously. Thus, he has no locus standee at all. He is just like a floating voter of any election in democracy set up.

**KEYWORDS:** Convince, persuade, satisfy, vanquish, overcome, confute, convict, refute

## INTRODUCTION

Creative writing is based more on manifestation rather than on expression. It does not inform, rather it reveals. So it bears no reference. The best creative writing is critical, and the best critical writing is creative. This article is an outcome of thinking about creative writing meant for a general readership. As such, I have adopted a free style methodology so that everyone can enjoy the pleasure of reading. As you might know, Francis Bacon (1561-1626), the immortal essayist, wrote many essays namely 'Of Love', 'Of Friendship', 'Of Ambition', 'Of Studies', and so on. The multiple-minded genius correctly pointed out that all the words of the dictionary can be used as themes for essays. But little has been done since his death to continue or finish his monumental task. Bacon's unique individual style of presentation ignited my imagination and encouraged me to write creative essays as a method of relieving a wide range of emotions through catharsis.

## ARTICLE

Convince is to cause somebody to believe that something is the case. For example: How can I convince you of her honesty? What she said convinced me that I had been wrong. It is to persuade somebody to do something. For example: What convinced you to vote for them?

Convince is to persuade by argument or proof e.g. to convince a person of his folly. It, now obsolete, is to prove or find guilty. It is to vanquish. It is to overcome, confute, or convict. It is to overcome the doubts of. It is to make feel sure.

Convince is to persuade a person to believe or realize firmly the truth. For example: I failed to convince him of his mistake. It is to overcome, get the better of. It is to subdue the mind of by evidence. It is to satisfy as to truth or error. As per Bible it is to convict. It, now obsolete, is to refute.

Convinced is completely sure about something. For example: I am convinced of her innocence/convinced that she is innocent. It is firm in one's belief e.g. a convinced Christian; a convinced pacifist.

Convincing is that makes somebody believe something or persuade somebody e.g. a convincing speech/argument/assurance/lie.

Convincing is causing one to feel sure or to believe or agree. It is persuading as by evidence. It is cogent. It is producing conviction. It is certain, positive, beyond doubt. It is by a large or significant margin.It is leaving no margin of doubt, substantial e.g. a convincing victory i.e. an easy one.

Convincingly means hope for positive outcome. For example: Her case was convincingly argued.

Convincement is especially of religious conviction.

Someone can convince. Someone can't. It is a personality trait. Pleasing personality accelerates it. Intelligence strengthens it.Wisdom confirms it. Beautiful face can convince easily. As such hero or heroine i.e. glamour world is used for promotional purpose while launching any new product.

All cannot convince. All cannot be convinced. Someone is convinced and benefit is obtained thereby. Someone is not convinced thereby favour remains out of reach. A self-status person seldom thinks for convincing. He always depends on his personal capacity. He contends that one can earn more by the time used for convincing. This strategy has immense impact upon the person who declined to be convinced. In future the person can be convinced easily. He will not enjoy sadistic pleasure declining the request further. Also he will think if he does not consider then the opponent will do without his help. Further his help will pave the way for future reciprocation.

A person is well advised not to be convinced without realizing the matter or manner.Then he can ask for time to think over the issue in question. If the person has lack of knowledge then he can take help either from a professional person or a well-wisher.

Before signing any contract the person in question should be convinced properly. Someone is convinced but declines to sign at the final moment. As such a vacillating character should be handled with utmost care and caution. So a wise person becomes sure and certain first then proceed for implementation of contract. Business and especially marriage convincement are very crucial. Otherwise all arrangement will be of no use except simply wastage of money and time as well.

An optimist considers convincement as positive venture. As such one should not be afraid before convincing any person. Obviously, outcome of convincing is confirmed only when argument is purely based on logic.

There are two types of persons. The first category is convinced easily. The second category is not convinced easily. The merit of first category is that he is convinced easily. The demerit of first category is that he is convinced easily. Such a dual character is so unique that he possesses both merit and demerit simultaneously. He is just like a floating voter of any election in democratic set up. Thus he is convinced by the campaign of the first political party. In the next very moment he is convinced by the second political party. In fact, he has no locus standee at all. As such his mood and motif are gloriously so uncertain. And the fate of any politician is determined by these voters. They are real king maker. As such even a shrewd politician fails to gauge the pulse of these unpredictable voters.

Different persons are convinced differently. Someone is convinced by logic. Someone is convinced by magic. Someone is convinced by none of these two options. Ugly person though wise cannot convince a heroine who is always convinced by a smart guy. Beautiful face can convince easily even a wise person. Here beauty is the convincing tool.

Again someone can be convinced by emotion. Someone is convinced by motion. Someone is convinced by sexual pleasure. Someone is convinced by bribe. Someone may be convinced either by cash or kind. Generally, an intelligent boss is so kind that he accepts only cash. He avoids the hazards of encashing any kind.

Someone pre-decides to be convinced. Someone pre-decides not to be convinced. Thus the second category is difficult to convince. For, it is difficult to make unwilling horse drink water.

## CONCLUSION

There are two types of friends viz., class friend and glass friend. The relation between two class friends may not last long. The paradox is that glass is brittle but the relation between two glass friends is permanent. For, a drunkard is convinced easily by a bottle of wine. Here lies the uniqueness of convince.

## REFERENCES

No reference, since the present article is an outcome of Creative Writing

# *OF EMINENCE*

## ABSTRACT

An important person is eminent. Also, an eminent person is important. Thus fame is alias and akin to eminence. Fame does not guarantee respect. But, respect confirms fame. Thus all respectable persons are famous, but all famous persons may not get respect. Where fame ends, respect begins. This is the essence of eminence.

**KEYWORDS:** Eminence, famous, respect, high station, rank, recognition, superiority, celebrity

## INTRODUCTION

Creative writing is based more on manifestation rather than on expression. It does not inform, rather it reveals. So it bears no reference. The best creative writing is critical, and the best critical writing is creative. This article is an outcome of thinking about creative writing meant for a general readership. As such, I have adopted a free style methodology so that everyone can enjoy the pleasure of reading. As you might know, Francis Bacon (1561-1626), the immortal essayist, wrote many essays namely 'Of Love', 'Of Friendship', 'Of Ambition', 'Of Studies', and so on. The multiple-minded genius correctly pointed out that all the words of the dictionary can be used as themes for essays. But little has been done since his death to continue or finish his monumental task. Bacon's unique individual style of presentation ignited my imagination and encouraged me to write creative essays as a method of relieving a wide range of emotions through catharsis.

## ARTICLE

Eminence is the state of being famous or respected in one's profession e.g. rise to/achieve/reach eminence as a doctor. It is high station, rank, or repute e.g. philosophers of eminence.

Eminence is a part eminent or rising above the rest. It is a piece of rising ground e.g. The villa stood on an eminence facing the east.

It is a ridge or knob. It is height. It is distinction. It is a title given in 1631 to cardinals, till then styled Most Illustrious. It is advantage, upper hand.

It is a high or lofty place or part, thing, etc. It is a hill or elevation e.g. a fortress on a rocky eminence. It is recognized superiority in rank, position, character, achievement, etc. It is greatness. It is celebrity. It is an important person. It is distinguished superiority in social, intellectual, etc. For example: His eminence enabled him to dictate to people. He attained great eminence as a poet/philosopher/musician.

It is the title of honour applied to a Roman Catholic Cardinal usually preceded by His or Yours e.g. His/Your Eminence; Their/Your Eminence.

Eminent is high in station, rank, or repute. It is distinguished, notable. It is eminent statesmen. It is conspicuous, signal, or noteworthy e.g. eminent fairness; a man of eminent courage. It is lofty. It is high. It is prominent. It is projecting. It is protruding. It is of qualities remarkable in degree.

Eminent is famous and respected in a profession e.g. an eminent architect; eminent as a scientist; a woman of eminent virtue. His son is only slightly less eminent.

Eminent is rising high above other things or place. It is standing high by comparison with others, as in rank or achievement. It is renowned. It is exalted in rank or office. It is remarkable. It is outstanding e.g. a man of eminent good sense. He is eminent for his munificence/learning.

In anatomy it is an elevation or projection, especially on a bone. It is a raised area, usually on the surface of a bone.

Eminently is very. It is obviously e.g. She seems eminently suitable for the job.

Prominent, celebrated, renowned, illustrious, outstanding, famous, noted, notable are synonymous with eminence.

Eminent domain, as per law, is the right of a government to take, or to authorize the taking of, private property for public use, just compensation being given to the owner. It is the right by which the supreme authority in a state may compel a proprietor to part with what is his own for the public use.

Eminence grise is a person who exercises power or influence without holding office. It is a confidential agent. It  is one exercising power in the background, as

Cardinal Richelieu's private secretary and alter ego Pere Joseph, nicknamed I' Eminence Grise i.e. 'the Grey Eminence'.

All cannot be eminent. It needs labour. It demands labour. Sincere and prolonged devotion strengthen it. Very few people can continue it. Not everyone can be the owner of such rare blessing. Very few fortunate people acquire it. Furthermore, devotion is akin to physical pain. Very few can bear it. This explains why we encounter so few people having eminence.

Eminence is a matter of lucky thing. Its use is in this mundane world. A person having this blessing is always ahead. Though it is mundane, only a blessed soul attains this divine favour. An unfortunate person can hardly think of it. Such a cursed victim faces misery from cradle to coffin. Only a rich or elite enjoys its warm feeling. This status smoothens real life. Then life becomes a bed of roses.

Eminence is a matter of luck. Two persons having equal merit may not be equally eminent. This happens in case of doctors, lawyers, teachers, and so on. Sometimes a person of mediocre  or less talent earns huge amount of money in comparison of other intellectuals around him and becomes so-called eminent. Here lies the mystery. Here lies the tragedy.

The children of eminent parents get bonus marks in real life. They are welcomed by all. They face no trouble. Also they earn eminence without being eminent in person. Thus they are born with recommendation that paves the way to attain success everywhere.

Eminence is a force. All cannot bear this psychological pressure. To an elite person it is quite normal. As such a member of an eminent family can tackle such a situation at ease. In contrast, a person hailing from low-socio economic society fails nerve if he gets huge amount of money from lottery and becomes eminent. He spends lavishly. He enjoys riotous living. Very soon he becomes poor again. Thus to such a degraded soul eminence is like a short story.

It is difficult to be eminent. It is more difficult to hold it for long. An eminent person may suffer from superiority complex. This feeling of superiority insists him to be proud. He acquires ill-fame for his haughty behavior. Pride goes before a fall. He experiences down-fall ultimately and untimely.

A wise person is eminent. He never misuses his power. He knows all is uncertain. Eminence is no exception. Today's eminent person may not be eminent tomorrow. He may lose it for his illegal activity or unlawful involvement.

Rome was not built in a day. Similarly, eminence can never be achieved overnight. It requires time for its settlement. As such an intelligent person prepares from the very beginning of his life to acquire eminence. One should not lose heart if he fails. He should try till he attains success.

Regarding success one should keep it in mind that if a person tries to achieve something there are two possibilities, either he may fail or he may fail to fail. A person should simply try for the later one. In fact, an optimist always follows the same. In contrast, a pessimist or a lazy person sits idle and curses his fate. Thus to them eminence is a matter of far-off land.

One should not be envious of any eminent person. Rather he should try to be eminent following the foot print of the successful eminent persons. Envy not only degrades the soul also it defames.

An eminent person is respected by all and everywhere. Also, an eminent person respects others as reciprocation. This good gesture adds another feather in his cap. Here lies his uniqueness. Here lies his eminence. That's why he is eminent.

Eminence is culture free. It breaks all barriers and crosses all boundaries with its noble essence. Some persons think that eminence is of the rich, by the rich and for the rich.  But in reality, a person of low birth can achieve it. In contrast an aristocrat person may lose it for having lackadaisical attitude. Thus eminence is not the monopoly of the elite society.

Money or wealth is not the yardstick of eminence. Personality trait like goodness thereby greatness is the chief ingredient of eminence. Such a person is the true celebrity.


## CONCLUSION

An important person is eminent. Also, an eminent person is important. Thus fame is alias and akin to eminence. Fame does not guarantee respect. But, respect confirms fame. Thus all respectable persons are famous, but all famous persons may not get respect. Where fame ends, respect begins. This is the essence of eminence.


## REFERENCES

No reference, since the present article is an outcome of Creative Writing

*OF EXTRA*

## ABSTRACT


Extra-curricular activity is an avenue to show the actual talent. It may be extra to a normal student. But it is main to a talented student. An independent scholar seldom goes to an Alma meter since traditional educational methodology is quite tedious to him. Stereotype syllabus bores him. He feels suffocated in such closed chamber. To him extra-curricular activity is very important. But the devotion of an independent scholar remains unevaluated. He becomes isolated. He is avoided by all. Thus he dies unpaid. He dies unfed. He dies unwept. He dies unsung. And he dies unknown as well like nameless thousands who built the pyramids.

**KEYWORDS:** Extra, more, beyond, additional, further, outside, extraordinary, unusual


## INTRODUCTION

Creative writing is based more on manifestation rather than on expression. It does not inform, rather it reveals. So it bears no reference. The best creative writing is critical, and the best critical writing is creative. This article is an outcome of thinking about creative writing meant for a general readership. As such, I have adopted a free style methodology so that everyone can enjoy the pleasure of reading. As you might know, Francis Bacon (1561-1626), the immortal essayist, wrote many essays namely 'Of Love', 'Of Friendship', 'Of Ambition', 'Of Studies', and so on. The multiple-minded genius correctly pointed out that all the words of the dictionary can be used as themes for essays. But little has been done since his death to continue or finish his monumental task. Bacon's unique individual style of presentation ignited my imagination and encouraged me to write creative essays as a method of relieving a wide range of emotions through catharsis.

## ARTICLE

Extra is more than or beyond what is usual, expected or necessary. It is additional e.g. demand extra pay for extra work; order an extra pint of milk. There were a few extra seats in the auditorium.The bus company provided extra buses because there were so many people. We need an extra $5 million a year to cover the costs of research. Place an extra burden on the taxpayer. Take extra care.

Extra is more than usually e.g. an extra-large helping of rice; extra fine quality. It is in addition e.g. earn a bit extra this month; charge/pay 20% extra; price $12, postage and packing extra.

Extra is an extra thing. It is a thing that costs extra e.g. a new car with all the extras. The price you pay for your excursion is the complete price; there are no hidden extras. School fees are $300 a term; music and dancing are optional extras.

Extra is a person employed to play a very small part, e.g. in a crowd scene. We need hundreds of extras for the battle scene.

Extra time, in sport, a further period of play at the end of a football match, etc. when the scores are equal at the end of the normal period.

Extra is outside. It is beyond e.g. extramarital; extracurricular. It is very. It is to an exceptional degree e.g. extra-thin; extra-special.

Extra is a prefix meaning 'outside', 'beyond', freely used as an English formative e.g. extrajudicial; extraterritorial.

Extra is extraordinary. It is unusually. What is extra or additional, as an item above and beyond the ordinary school curriculum, something over and above the usual course or charge in a bill, etc. It is a special edition of a newspaper containing later news. It is a run scored at cricket from a bye, leg-bye, wide, or no-ball i.e. not hit.

Extra is prefix meaning outside, outside the scope or region of, beyond, besides. It is added to adjectives. The list below contains some common compounds formed with this prefix that do not have special meanings: extracellular, extra continental, extracorporeal, extra cranial, extra familial, extra governmental, extra hepatic, extra historic, extra linguistic, extra official, extra planetary, extraprofessional, extra social, extra solar,extraterrestrial.

Extra is outside.

Extra size is outsize.

Extra-base hit, in baseball, is any hit greater than a single. It is double, triple, or home run.

Extrabold, in printing, is a style of type heavier than boldface.

Extracanonical is not included in the canon of the Bible. It is not among the authorized books.

Extracellular, in biology, is situated or taking place outside a cell or cells.

Extra dry is of champagne very slightly sweetened.

Extra atmospheric is of the space beyond the atmosphere.

Extra cranial is outside the skull.

Extra illustrate is add pictures to book from another source.

Extra judicial is not belonging to the case before the court, not legally authorized e.g. of confession, not made in court. Thus it is beyond the usual course of legal proceeding.

Extramarital is of sexual relationships outside marriage.

Extraterrestrial is outside the earth or its atmosphere.

Extra-condensed, in print, is narrower than condensed type in proportion to its height.

Extra cover, in cricket, is a fielding position between cover point and mid-off, or the player in this position.

Extra-curricular is of a subject or activity, outside and additional to the regular academic course.

Extra-illustrate is to grangerise.

Extra-special is much out of the way. It is a special late edition of an evening newspaper called for by some news of great importance.

Extra time is additional time allowed at the end of a match because of time lost through injury, or for other reason.

Extra modum is beyond measure, extravagant.

Extra muros is beyond the walls.

Extra-axillary is not in the axil of a leaf.

Extracorporeal is outside the body.

Extradotal is not forming part of the dowry.

Extrafloral is not in a flower.

Extraforaneous is out-door.

Extragalactic is outside the Milky Way.

Extralimital is not found within a given faunal area. It is lying outside a prescribed area.

Extrametrical is in excess of the recognized number of syllables in the line.

Extramundane is beyond the material world or the universe.

Extramural is without or beyond the walls. It is connected with a university but not under its direct control.

Extranuclear is outside the nucleus of a shell.

Extraparochial is beyond the limits of a parish.

Extraphysical is not subject to physical laws.

Extraprofessional is not belonging to a particular profession. It is outside the usual limits of professional duty or practice.

Extraprovincial is outside the limits of a particular province.

Extraregular is unlimited by rules.

Extrasensory is outside the ordinary senses as in clairvoyant and telepathic perception. It is the ability to perceive without the normal senses i.e. sixth sense.

Extrasolar is beyond the solar system.

Extraterritorial is outside a territory or territorial jurisdiction.

Extraterritoriality is the privilege of being outside the jurisdiction of the country one is in.

Extratropical is outside the tropics.

Extrauterine is outside the uterus.

Extravascular is outside the vascular system or a vessel. It is not vascular.

Extravehicularis outside a vehicle .It is situated, used, or happening, especially outside a spacecraft.

A student is bound to complete the regular academic course to build the career. Most of the students follow that avenue. They don't want to take any kind of risk. They are afraid of diversion. They don't want to be diverted genius. They don't want to be misguided missile. But some genius persons get no interest in traditional academic field for its stereo and tedious methodology.

Extra-curricular activity is an avenue to show the actual talent. It may be extra to a normal student. But it is main to a talented student. An independent scholar seldom goes to an Alma meter since traditional educational methodology is quite tedious to him. Stereotype syllabus bores him. He feels suffocated in such closed chamber. To him extra-curricular activity is very important. But the devotion of an independent scholar remains unevaluated. He becomes isolated. He is avoided by all. Thus he dies unpaid. He dies unfed. He dies unwept. He dies unsung. And he dies unknown as well like nameless thousands who built the pyramids.

An inattentive student is more interested in extra-curricular activity which seldom pays. He wastes valuable time of student life. Man realizes his wrong devotion when he reaches the autumn of life. Then he has nothing to do except mourning. In fact every moment of student life is precious. If a student wastes a single moment of that crucial period of life then thousand moments of future hardly can compensate that deficiency.

Extra-precautionary measures should always be taken in school, office, auditorium, cinema hall, etc. i.e. public places where danger may appear at any time.Some cautious parents take extra-precautionary measures for their children for full blooming.

If the thing is good a person is ready to pay extra charge. A person pays extra charge in crisis period. A lover is always ready to pay extra charges for a ticket for his fiancée to enjoy the movie together.

Extra allowance encourages to work in extra time. A corrupted person sits idle in working hours. He becomes active after office is over. Then he demands extra charge for extra work which in fact is normal work. Perks are the greatest example of extra allowance. The funny thing is that this allowance is more than basic pay. The company tames the employees with this financial tool.

Perks are given to the employees to avoid income tax. The company thinks that it is better to pay surplus money to the employees rather than paying the government as income tax. The employees are happy with this special benefit. The company knows well that it is difficult to make unwilling horse drink water.

What is extra may not be extra or additional if it is used properly. In fact extra is an assumption which is due to lacking in knowledge for present or future use. A wise person never considers anything extra rather the learned keeps that thing with care as a blessing.

Extra is good if it favours. It is too bad if it favours not. Then it is a liability. Hidden cost is an extra burden. A dishonest travel agent does not disclose the hidden cost before commencing of the journey. He demands extra money thereby squeezes the tourist in the mid-way. As a result the joy and merriment of the whole tour program becomes a threat only instead.

Condition apply in marketing is an extra danger. This caution is printed in the package of any product or application for a share to avoid any legal action from the consumer or shareholder. This caution is not to draw attention rather is printed in the lowest possible font so that a person hardly notices it. This is a tricky game played by the companies.

A commodity has its original price. Delivery charge is extra. Some companies bear this charge as apromotional strategy. When the product enjoys much demand then delivery charge is imposed upon the customer. A customer is ready to purchase a costly product with higher price. The paradox is that that very customer declines to pay the delivery charge. A person spends much extra money in many places for many extra occasions in many modes in many manners. But that very person bargains for rickshaw or vehicle fair. It is a common psychology of the customer known by the companies.

The seat rent of any hotel is fixed. But breakfast and meals are extras. A hotel owner does not know the quantity of consumptions of food of any tourist. As such he does not take the risk of eating and drinking. Some hotel managers charge higher price for accommodation. They provide free breakfast. To avoid embarrassing situations they show the printed menu chart of the breakfast during booking.

After sales service is never obtained from a salesman during warranty period. The machine becomes defunct just after warranty period is over. The repairing cost is nearly the price of the new product. One repairing is followed by another one. Then it is judicious to purchase a new machine instead of repairing. The companies also insist accordingly. It is just like use and throw policy. It is an extra cheating business of the industrialist. They say if a product lasts long then the production unit will be collapsed and the labourers will be jobless.

Extra marital affair is the worst example of extra. A married person is involved in extra marital affair if the partner fails to satisfy sexual urge or there is lack in intimacy. Also some persons become involved in extra marital affair even there is no deficiency in sex and love. They are either habitual offender or addicted person. A wise person never becomes involved in such dirty game thinking social status or future of the innocent sons and daughters. The children are its worst victim.

Extra judicial is an avenue for relief to both plaintiff and defendant. Initially, both the parties fight to satisfy ego, hatred and anger. Provocation refrains them form coming to any settlement. Later on, when hair becomes grey, eye-sight becomes feeble then both the rivals realize that justice is a matter of far-off land. Then they compromise outside court.

Extraordinary is very important and valued much in every sphere of life. This attribute is possessed by only a blessed soul. Extraordinary brilliant student is an asset of any academic institution. A sharp shooter possesses this quality and enjoys much demand in hunting and war as well. A skilled worker earns much for his extraordinary expertise. A surgeon has to attain extraordinary expertise for difficult surgical operations.

Lack in knowledge of proper budget gives birth either of shortage or extra. Extra thing or extra person causes extra expenditure. An intelligent and experienced person takes extra money to meet up the unexpected expenditure in new place or environment. In contrast a fool or a miser goes out with exact amount of money lest extra money is spent. Now, if the price of the thing is increased then it cannot buy for want of money. Again if the fare of the vehicle is more than before then it cannot avail the vehicle for journey. As such extra has its both merit and demerit.

Generally, there is a common arrangement for people from all walks of life. Also there is extra facility. This facility is offered for patient, senior-citizen or sophisticated elite person. A person is ready to pay extra money if extra benefit is obtained. This is just like AC and Non AC of hotel room.

Extra illustrations or examples enrich any writing. Extra meal satisfies a hungry person. Extra classes pave the way to finish the syllabus in or before time of any academic institution. These extra classes strengthen the solid foundation of the students. Optional or extra subjects enhance to build the career.

An extra person earns very little that is quite insufficient for livelihood. Though he is extra he has no extra income. The paradox is that only a rich has many extra avenues for extra income. It seems one extra income encourages thereby paves the way for another extra income and so on. It is a chain process. In this way once a poor person becomes rich within a short period of time.In contrast a poor person has no extra income. Even his only single income is closed for his lack of intelligence.

## CONCLUSION

In any examination extra of geometry is a difficult problem. Only an extraordinary student can attempt it. This extra merit gauzes the extra caliber of the concerned student.

## REFERENCES

No reference, since the present article is an outcome of Creative Writing

# *OF FRANK*

## ABSTRACT

An extrovert is frank. He speaks all. He speaks to all. He is popular. Everybody loves him. Nobody is afraid of him. In contrast, an introvert is unfrank. He is of reserve personality. He speaks nothing. He speaks to none. He keeps mum. He practices to be mum. He speaks if he likes. He speaks not, if he likes not. Thus his mood and motive are gloriously so uncertain. As such he is not popular. Nobody loves him. Everybody is afraid of him. Thus to an extrovert if frankness is classical success then to an introvert unfrankness is artistic failure.

**KEYWORDS:** Frank, free, open, honest, direct, unreserved, straightforward, evident, plain

## INTRODUCTION

Creative writing is based more on manifestation rather than on expression. It does not inform, rather it reveals. So it bears no reference. The best creative writing is critical, and the best critical writing is creative. This article is an outcome of thinking about creative writing meant for a general readership. As such, I have adopted a free style methodology so that everyone can enjoy the pleasure of reading. As you might know, Francis Bacon (1561-1626), the immortal essayist, wrote many essays namely 'Of Love', 'Of Friendship', 'Of Ambition', 'Of Studies', and so on. The multiple-minded genius correctly pointed out that all the words of the dictionary can be used as themes for essays. But little has been done since his death to continue or finish his monumental task. Bacon's unique individual style of presentation ignited my imagination and encouraged me to write creative essays as a method of relieving a wide range of emotions through catharsis.

# ARTICLE

Frank is free, open, honest and direct in speech or writing. It is unreserved in speech e.g. a frank reply/discussion/exchange of views.

It is straightforward. It is free from reserve, disguise, or guile. It is clearly evident. It is plain e.g. showing frank distaste. It is unrestrained.

It is open and honest in expressing what one thinks or feels. For example: To be perfectly frank with you, I think your son has little chance of passing the examination.

It is candid or outspoken e.g. a frank opinion; frank admiration; frank diabetes.It is sincere. It is without inhibition or subterfuge. It is direct. It is undisguised, avowed e.g.a frank appeal to base motives. It is ingenuous, open e.g. a frank face/statement. In medieval medicine it is unmistakable.

Archaic logically, it is liberal or generous. Obviously, it is free in giving.

Frankly is speaking honestly. It is to be truthful e.g. Frankly, I could not care less what happens to him. Quite frankly, I am not surprised he failed.

Frankly is to be frank. It is in a frank manner. For example: She expressed her opinions fully and frankly.Frankly, you don't have a chance.

Frankness means plainness of speech e.g. She spoke about her fears with complete/disarming frankness.It is the quality of being open and honest. It is telling the truth, even when it is painful to do so.

Further frank is to mark letters, etc., with an official stamp, other than a postage stamp, indicating payment of postage.With historical reference it is to superscribe a letter etc. with a signature ensuring conveyance without charge.Thus, it is to exempt from future payment etc. e.g. a franking duty, imposition.

It is to sign so as to ensure free carriage. It is to send thus signed. It is to send mail free of postage, as by virtue of an official position. It is to mark by means of a franking machine to show that postage has been paid. It is the signature of a person who had the right to frank a letter. It is a franked cover.

It is to mark mail as with one's signature so that it can be sent free. It is to put a stamp on or meter mail to prepay postage. It is the privilege of sending mail free. It is a mark, signature, or stamp on mail for, or in place of, postage. It is an envelope, etc. that has been franked.

It is to stamp a mark on a letter, etc. to show that the cost of posting has been paid or does not need to be paid. It is a signature or mark affixed by special privilege to a letter, package, or the like, to ensure free transmission. It is the privilege of franking letters, packages, etc. It is a franked letter, package, etc. It is to mark a letter, package, etc. for free transmission. It is to send free of charge.

It is to make easy the passage of a person. It is to convey a person free of charge. It is to enable to pass or go freely e.g. to frank a visitor through customs. In archaic it is to facilitate the coming and going of a person thereby give social passport to.

Frank, candid, open and outspoken are synonymous.

Free, bold, uninhibited are synonyms with frank.

Frank, candid, open, outspoken imply a freedom and boldness in speaking.

Frank is applied to a person unreserved in expressing the truth and his real opinions and sentiments e.g. a frank analysis of a personal problem. It applies to a person, remark, etc. that is free or blunt in expressing the truth or an opinion, unhampered by conventional reticence e.g. a frank criticism.

Candid suggests that a person is sincere and truthful or impartial and fair in judgement, sometimes unpleasantly so e.g. a candid expression of opinion.It implies a basic honesty that makes deceit or evasion impossible, sometimes to the embarrassment of the listener e.g. a candid opinion.

Open implies a lack of reserve e.g. open antagonism. It implies a lack of concealment and often connotes an ingenuous quality e.g. her open admiration for him.

Outspoken applies to a person who expresses himself freely, even when this is inappropriate e.g. an outspoken criticism. It suggests a lack of restraint or reserve in speech, especially when reticence might be preferable.

Frank is informal and colloquially, frankfurter.

Frank is a masculine name. It is the diminished form of Frankie.

Robert Frank, an U.S. photographer, was born in Switzerland.

Frank is a member of a group of ancient Germanic peoples dwelling in the regions of the Rhine, one division of whom, the Salians, conquered Gaul about A.D. 500. It is a member of the Germanic tribes that established the Frankish Empire, which, at its height i.e. beginning of the 9$^{th}$ cent A.D extended over what is now, France, Germany, and Italy. It is, in the eastern Mediterranean region, a person of Western nationality.

Frank is abbreviated of Frankish.

Frank is in the Levant any native or inhabitant of Western Europe.

Frank fee is tenure in fee-simple.

Frank pledge is a mutual suretyship by which the members of a tithing were made responsible for one another.

Frank tenement is freehold.

Frank is a pigsty. It is to shut up in a sty. It is to cram, to fatten.

Frank is Anne (1929-45), German Jewish girl. Her diary (1947; The Diary of a Young Girl, 1953) records the experiences of her family living for two years in hiding from the Nazis in occupied Amsterdam. They were eventually betrayed and sent to concentration camps. Anne died in Belsen. Her diary has been translated into over thirty languages.

Two talkative persons or two frank persons match well. They either are made for each other or mad for each other or both simultaneously. People around them feel disturbance hearing their continuous dialogues. Their eloquence renders public annoyed. But they don't bother. They express and exchange their violent emotions untiringly. None can bind them. No force can resist them.

Frank person is talkative. He is liked by another talkative person. He gets relief through expressing. But he is disliked by a reserve personality. As such a frank person should speak accordingly.

Frank person is good with rigidity. Frank person is too bad with tenderness. He is unfit as an administrator. Also such a person is not fit for the hotel manager. In a hotel people from all walks of life come for staying and enjoyment. A manager has to tackle all the customers having various mood and motive.

Frankness is a rare virtue. Only a truthful person can speak frankly. He seldom thinks for future consequences, since he is ready to face any situation. He will always speak the truth even in the changed situation inspite of its severity.

To be frank needs stamina. It demands courage. Such a person plays in a straight bat. Only a blessed soul can attain this personality trait.

A selfish person cannot be frank. He always thinks for profit of any action. He thinks for future consequences. He never speaks the truth. He always tells lies. His different cocktail statements of lies contradict with each other. As such he cannot thereby does not play in a straight bat.

A child is frank. A fool is frank. An honest person is frank. A poor person is frank. A rich is not frank. A cheater is not frank. It pretends to be frank to cheat.

Always frankness is not wise. A fool is frank when not to be and it becomes eloquent when to keep mum thus loses both ways.

A frank person is not suitable for confidential job or secret communication. He is not fit for privacy. If, inadvertently, such an extrovert character is engaged as a confidential assistant then he will do all works except confidential job so confidently that the flood gate of the secret matters of the organization is opened and the opponent party will collect all information from him at ease.

In diplomacy there is criticality if both the parties involved are of same power. Then problem remains unsolved. Now for permanent solution frank discussion suits well. A criticality cannot substitute another criticality; rather the situation becomes more critical. But frankness can be substitute of criticality. Here lies the uniqueness of frankness.

Man becomes frank when death is imminent. Dying declaration is frank. During alive when a person is physically fit, mentally sound and economically strong he is critical. These are bar of frankness. But wise is always frank. Wealth cannot render him critical.


## CONCLUSION

An extrovert is frank. He speaks all. He speaks to all. He is popular. Everybody loves him. Nobody is afraid of him. In contrast, an introvert is unfrank. He is of reserve personality. He speaks nothing. He speaks to none. He keeps mum. He practices to be mum. He speaks if he likes. He speaks not, if he likes not. Thus his mood and motive are gloriously so uncertain. As such he is not popular. Nobody loves him. Everybody is afraid of him. Thus to an extrovert if frankness is classical success then to an introvert unfrankness is artistic failure.

# REFERENCES

No reference, since the present article is an outcome of Creative Writing

## *OF INCOMPLETE*


**ABSTRACT**

If an author dies leaving any writing incomplete, then different critics conclude differently as per their sweet will. It is their democratic right they get without any agitation but by default. Sometimes an author does not conclude for the sake of art. But some critics interpret in such a way that the author did not actually mean what the critics meant. Sometimes a critic opines the opposite view or a completely new and innovative one which the author did not think in dream even. Here lies the glory of criticism. Here lies the consequence of incompleteness.

**KEYWORDS:** Incomplete, lacking, unfinished, imperfect


## INTRODUCTION

Creative writing is based more on manifestation rather than on expression. It does not inform, rather it reveals. So it bears no reference. The best creative writing is critical, and the best critical writing is creative. This article is an outcome of thinking about creative writing meant for a general readership. As such, I have adopted a free style methodology so that everyone can enjoy the pleasure of reading. As you might know, Francis Bacon (1561-1626), the immortal essayist, wrote many essays namely 'Of Love', 'Of Friendship', 'Of Ambition', 'Of Studies', and so on. The multiple-minded genius correctly pointed out that all the words of the dictionary can be used as themes for essays. But little has been done since his death to continue or finish his monumental task. Bacon's unique individual style of presentation ignited my imagination and encouraged me to write creative essays as a method of relieving a wide range of emotions through catharsis.

# ARTICLE

Incomplete is not having all its parts. It is lacking some parts. It is lacking a part or parts. It is not whole. It is not full. It is unfinished. It is not concluded. It is imperfect. It is not thorough.

Incomplete is not complete e.g. an incomplete set of figures. In football, it is of a forward pass not having been completed. It is not caught by a receiver. In botany it is wanting calyx, corolla, or both.

Someone laments for being his works incomplete. A pious soul laments not. The learned considers it as being inevitable and unconquerable destiny as desired by the Almighty.

Someone gets little remuneration due to incomplete work. If he has less demand then he is satisfied. If he has higher demand then he is unhappy. Thus someone tries and be satisfied whatever he gets. He loves him much than ambition. Those who love ambition hanker after it. Lover hankers after lover madly. Ambitious person runs after ambition badly. Both fail and lament sadly.

Whenever someone tries to achieve something there are two possibilities. Either the person may fail or the person may fail to fail. A person should simply try for the latter one.

Someone dies mature but did little. Someone dies premature but contributed much. Now, in both the cases whether life is complete or incomplete is a million dollar question. Incomplete is a matter of perception. This perception is not unique. As such perception varies person to person. Also it varies with the socio-economic status, education, culture of the concerned person alongwith time, place, etc.

Time is short. As such a person cannot complete. Time management is very important. Someone wastes much time in trifling or unimportant matters. He pays much attention where not to pay and pays no attention at all where to pay much thus loses both ways.

Tact of omission is an art. This omission saves time thereby a person completes work timely and sometimes before time. Some persons are active and follow 'do it' now policy. The very word pending is absent in their dictionary. To them pending means decline. Pending works are done never. 'Now or never' is their policy. They hate incompleteness.

A wise uses time judiciously. He  is vigilant for every moment of life with utmost care. He knows the value of time. He knows better that time is the most precious ingredient of life that determines human destiny. As such he follows time management very cautiously. Time is not a commodity. The learned knows that money can be earned seldom time. He knows that time and tide waits for none. Everybody repents for loss of time. A student contends that if he would get few more minutes he would complete the incomplete answer.

Student life is the most important time of any person. If a single moment of student life is misused then thousand moments of future can hardly compensate that deficiency. Due to wastage of time a student cannot complete his study. With incomplete bio data he gets no job. He remains unemployed. Misfortune dogs him wherever he goes. Misfortune follows him like shadow till he breadths his last.

A fool wastes time callously for having no planning at all. Planning means thinking before doing. Most of its works are incomplete due to proper planning. Common people start all and everything and leave in the mid-way either half done or part done or completely undone. As such they say look before you leap. A person should commit only which he can keep.

Incomplete is like under finance. In case of underfinance whole amount of money thus invested so far is simply wastage having no return. It is a trap to a novice entrepreneur who has to pay interest of financial loan. As such under finance is better than no finance at all. Before starting any work one should think whether the assignment is within his limit or beyond his limit or beyond his jurisdiction or beyond his capacity. Otherwise life will be infested with incompleteness.

One wastes valuable time and laments for incomplete works. Some communities finish early. Someone is lethargic in nature. Late Lateef is always late in completion. All tries few succeed. Failure is alias and akin to incomplete job. Some people fail and leave the work undone.

Incompleteness is curse. Finishing is blessing. Only a blessed soul can finish or attain success. Both expertise and luck are must to finish anything.

One must find the cause of completion. If he can find the cause of completion then he can also find the cause of incompletion. Only a knowledgeable person having thorough knowledge can complete in time and also can find the cause of incompleteness. Someone is expert in objective. Someone has mastery in subjective. Both fail in the opposite fields having incomplete outcome. Here all-rounder reaches the goal.

Someone argues that man must die so there is no difference between complete and incomplete work. A pious soul surrenders to god. To the wise both success and failure are equal and at par. A materialistic person thinks differently. He contends that man is mortal. Everybody knows it. It is a very important news. He pleads for the more important news that this very life is only for once. As such one should live properly and drink life to the lees. One should not be anxious and be captive in the hand of frustration till he exists.

Some frustrated lovers believe in rebirth and intend to meet in next life. Such an emotional person wants to finish his unfinished monumental incomplete works in next life either alone or jointly with his fiancée.

An examinee may not finish and submits answer script incomplete. Someone writes all answers but incomplete in nature. Someone leaves whole question. An intelligent student writes all answers in brief thereby completes though incomplete style while the time is short .

## CONCLUSION

If an author dies leaving any writing incomplete, then different critics conclude differently as per their sweet will. It is their democratic right they get without any agitation but by default. Sometimes an author does not conclude for the sake of art. But some critics interpret in such a way that the author did not actually mean what the critics meant. Sometimes a critic opines the opposite view or a completely new and innovative one which the author did not think in dream even. Here lies the glory of criticism. Here lies the consequence of incompleteness.

## REFERENCES

No reference, since the present article is an outcome of Creative Writing

# *OF OVERLOOK*

## ABSTRACT

Someone overlooks. Someone overlooks not. Both are personality traits. Someone overlooks to indulge. Someone overlooks not and indulges not. These also are personality traits. Someone controls wrongs and injustice with severity. It is another type of personality trait. It controls the nuisance. From overlooking socio-cultural status of the concerned person is identified. Also from overlooking talent and temperament are also ascertained. A wise knows what to overlook. He knows better what not to overlook. It is the outcome of talent. Also reaction aroused from any event is the outcome of temperament.

**KEYWORDS:** Overlook, miss, disregard, ignore, indulge, neglect, pass

## INTRODUCTION

Creative writing is based more on manifestation rather than on expression. It does not inform, rather it reveals. So it bears no reference. The best creative writing is critical, and the best critical writing is creative. This article is an outcome of thinking about creative writing meant for a general readership. As such, I have adopted a free style methodology so that everyone can enjoy the pleasure of reading. As you might know, Francis Bacon (1561-1626), the immortal essayist, wrote many essays namely 'Of Love', 'Of Friendship', 'Of Ambition', 'Of Studies', and so on. The multiple-minded genius correctly pointed out that all the words of the dictionary can be used as themes for essays. But little has been done since his death to continue or finish his monumental task. Bacon's unique individual style of presentation ignited my imagination and encouraged me to write creative essays as a method of relieving a wide range of emotions through catharsis.

# ARTICLE

Overlook is to fail to see or notice, perceive, or consider something. It is to miss something e.g. a fact that is all too easily overlooked. It is to disregard or ignore indulgently, as faults, misconduct, etc. It is to neglect. Thus, it is to ignore, condone an offence etc.

It is to view carefully.It is to pass by without cognizance or punishment. It is to see a mistake, wrongdoing, etc. but decide officially to ignore it. Thus, it is to take no notice of, allow offence to go unpunished.  For example: We can't afford to overlook such serious offences.

It is to consider somebody/something not good or important enough and so ignore them/it. For example: Despite her qualifications she has been repeatedly overlooked for the job.The boss always overlooks her faults. His claim to promotion has long been overlooked.

It is to rise above. It is to look at from above. It is to see from a higher position. It is a height from which to view surroundings. Also, it is the view. It is over top. It is to look over or beyond and not see.It is to have or give a view of a place from above it e.g. a flat overlooking Central Park; from a house overlooking the valley.Our garden is overlooked by our neighbours' windows.

It is to excuse. It is to slight. It is to pardon. It is to look over in inspection, examination, or perusal. It is to look after, oversee, or supervise.

In archaeology, it is to bewitch by looking upon with the evil eye.It is terrain, as on a cliff, that affords a view.In US it is a commanding position or view.

A over looker is a person who superintends, oversees.

The matter of children should not be overlooked. One may overlook when the person is adult or have the capacity to rectify. They have base. They have brake.They know what to tell. They know better what not to tell. They know where to stop, when to stop and how to stop. Thus conclusion thereby to conclude wisely is the business of a wise, seldom of a fool.

But children have nothing. So they should be guided properly. Otherwise, they become either illiterate or prodigal or both simultaneously. Later on, when the children grow up and face misery then they blame their parents. The teacher advises, "If you want to shine in life, don't find fault with others; rather find fault with yourself". Very few pupils follow it.

Man realizes the consequences of overlooking when he reaches the autumn of life. At that belated period neither the parents nor the grown up men have nothing to do except repentance and mourning. Man curses his parents. Parents curse themselves.

Overlook is a fault.Callous person overlooks. Serious person seldom overlooks. A wise person knows well the consequences of this omission. In case of private matter the concerned person is not answerable to anybody. But in case of public matter it brings the charge of negligence of duty. In both the cases the person and the dependent members of the family suffer. If the person is the only earning member of the family then the situation becomes severe.

Overlook may be either intentional or by mistake. Mistake may be corrected. Intentional may be either for mere indulgence or watch and wait policy for the right moment to take action.

If a person overlooks any obstruction on the way he stumbles. If someone searches for any lost thing and overlooks the same he seldom gets it back. Similarly, if the fiancée is lost in the crowd and the fiancé overlooks her presence then she is simply whisked away by his rival. Thus man willy-nilly overlooks many things or many matters from cradle to coffin. In this regard he is quite undone except experiencing loss and pain.

Overlook saves time. It is not wise to be involved in silly matters thereby waste time. Also it is not wise to be involved in the affairs of juniors or sub-ordinate staffs who respect. Obviously, if someone tries to insult or shows haughty behavior then action must have to be taken to keep up the status and to protect the chastity of the society.

It is bad to overlook. It is too bad to pay attention over a trifling matter. Then it will be presumed that it was far better to overlook. Also, a person becomes angry if minor matters get over attention.

Some persons do not overlook. They catch the matter instant, rebuke the persons involved and set them free with the bipartite commitment that he will not disclose the matter publicly and the wrongs must not recur anymore by the wrong doer. He is popular to all. He is respected by all.

Some persons look and pretend to overlook. He overlooks if the situation is not proper. Everything demands time and place for its occurrence. He asks the persons to rectify conduct and attitude. He pardons. He is a Good Samaritan. Again, someone blackmails the person involved.

If a person overlooks thereby indulges the crime then in future that crime returns back as boomerang. Thus he is paid by his own coin, since crime does not pay. And the wage of sin is death. Man realizes this in exchange of his valuable life.

Man looks. Man overlooks. Thus in the light of look and overlook the whole population may broadly be classified into four different categories.

The first type overlooks everything. Whether the matter is important or unimportant it matters little. He seldom cares for it. Thus he overlooks all and everything. It is his democratic right. He is happy with this right having no tension. The paradox is that all his neighbours do suffer from tension. It is his classical success that he has successfully transferred all his mundane anxieties to his well-wishers.

The second type overlooks if the matter is third party's affair. He is busy with his own business round the clock. He is so self-centered.

The third type overlooks nothing. He is so serious. He is a thorough person. It is not his personal gain. He has dedicated his life for public gain. He is a self-proclaimed patriot. He is afraid of none. Rather, everybody is afraid of him.

The fourth type overlooks, what to look and looks, what to overlook. Thus he loses both ways. None laughs for him. Rather everybody laughs at him.

Tact of omission is a great expertise. It depends upon prudence. In some case overlook acts as a tonic for better output. The person becomes obedient. He corrects himself. Thus sanctity of the relation between guilty and pardoner is maintained.

Someone overlooks. Someone overlooks not. Both are personality traits. Someone overlooks to indulge. Someone overlooks not and indulges not. These also are personality traits. Someone controls wrongs and injustice with severity. It is another type of personality trait. It controls the nuisance. From overlooking socio cultural status of the concerned person is identified. Also from overlooking talent and temperament are also ascertained. A wise knows what to overlook. He knows better what not to overlook. It is the outcome of talent. Also reaction aroused from any event is the outcome of temperament.

**CONCLUSION**

To look or not to look and to overlook or not to overlook is a very difficult question.

**REFERENCES**

No reference, since the present article is an outcome of Creative Writing

# *OF POLICY*

## ABSTRACT

There are numerous policies. Honesty is a policy. Dishonesty is also a policy. Cheating is a policy. Betray is also a policy. Similarly steal, ignore, hate, envy, hooliganism, etc. to name a few of different policies. All are professions. Different people are engaged in different professions accordingly as per their talent and temperament. All are unique in their respective aim and operation. But all has single agenda i.e. profit.

**KEYWORDS:** Policy, ideals, procedure, constitution, art, contract

## INTRODUCTION

Creative writing is based more on manifestation rather than on expression. It does not inform, rather it reveals. So it bears no reference. The best creative writing is critical, and the best critical writing is creative. This article is an outcome of thinking about creative writing meant for a general readership. As such, I have adopted a free style methodology so that everyone can enjoy the pleasure of reading. As you might know, Francis Bacon (1561-1626), the immortal essayist, wrote many essays namely 'Of Love', 'Of Friendship', 'Of Ambition', 'Of Studies', and so on. The multiple-minded genius correctly pointed out that all the words of the dictionary can be used as themes for essays.But little has been done since his death to continue or finish his monumental task. Bacon's unique individual style of presentation ignited my imagination and encouraged me to write creative essays as a method of relieving a wide range of emotions through catharsis.

## ARTICLE

Policy is a plan of action, statement of ideals, etc. proposed or adopted by a government, political party, business, etc., e.g. according to our present policy;

adopt fresh policies; US foreign/economic/domestic policy of the ministry; a policy-making body. What is the Labour Party's policy on immigration?

Policy is a definite course of action adopted for the sake of expediency, facility, etc. It is action or procedure conforming to or considered with reference to prudence or expediency. It is prudence, practical wisdom, or expediency.

Policy originally is government or polity.  It is now rare, political wisdom or cunning. It is wise, expedient, or prudent, sensible conduct or management. It is sagacity. It is any governing principle, plan, or course of action, as pursued by a government, organization, individual, etc. e.g. foreign policy; honesty is the best policy.

Policy is a constitution now obsolete. It is the art of government. It is statecraft. In archaeology, it is craftiness. It is a course of action. It is a system of administration guided more by interest than by principle. It is dexterity of management. In Scotland it is the pleasure-grounds around a mansion.It is park round country seat etc.

Policy is a written contract in which one party guarantees to insure another against a specified loss, damage, injury, etc. in consideration of payments, usually periodic, called premiums e.g. in full insurance policy.

It is the terms of a contract of insurance, or a written statement of this e.g. a fire insurance policy; a policy document.

In U.S it is a method of gambling in which bets are made on numbers to be drawn by lottery. It is numbers game.

Policy holder is the individual or firm in whose name an insurance policy is issued. It is an insured.

Policy is an illegal lottery in which winning numbers are drawn from a revolving drum. It is the numbers.

Policy loan is insurance, a loan made by a life insurance company to a policy holder with the cash value of his policy serving as security.

Policy shop is a place where the game of policy is played.

Strategy, principle, rules, acumen, astuteness are synonymous with policy.

Naiveté is the antonym of policy.

Policy is alias and akin to aim or objective. A person without aim is just like a ship without radar. An aero plane or a ship cannot reach its destination without radar. As such every person must have policy.

A tree is known by its fruit. Likewise, a person is known from his policy. Obviously, a true gentleman obeys the policy what he says. In contrast a critical person does not follow the policy as declared by him before doing any job.

He who follows policy shines in life. He can track the right avenue. Also he can be tracked. But a non-policy holder follows no definite track. As such he cannot be tracked. He has no locusstandi at all. He follows that path that has definite return. ROI i.e. return on investment is his policy.He thinks something. He does another thing. He declines his doings. He forgets all and everything. His contribution is nil. But his income is cent percent.

Policy is an art. All is not artist. All cannot be artist. It demands talent. It needs tenacity. Not everyone can be the owner of such rare power. Very few fortunate people acquire it. This explains why we encounter so few people with true policy.

An insurance policy saves life. In case of death or accident it saves mostly the family of common people. Common people suffer most due to lack of awareness of insurance policy. As such they say common sense is most uncommon among the common people.

There are numerous policies. Honesty is a policy. Dishonesty is also a policy. Cheating is a policy. Betray is also a policy. Similarly steal, ignore, hate, envy, hooliganism, etc. to name a few of different policies. All are professions. Different people are engaged in different professions accordingly as per their talent and temperament. All are unique in their respective aim and operation. But all has single agenda i.e. profit.

We may hate a thief. We may avoid them. But we cannot decline their existence. A thief has also a policy. He has a philosophy towards life which one may not agree. They say no politics is also a politics. Similarly, no policy is also a policy which is more than a policy. Thus different persons exist with different policies i.e., objectives towards life.

They say, honesty is the best policy.It is the best principle for people to live by. One may lie and remain unpunished. One speaks the truth but punished. But an honest person wins in the long run. Honesty is the policy of wise. Honesty is the easiest way to an honest person. But to a dishonest person honesty is next to impossible. A dishonest person hardly can think of honesty even in dream. Wages of sin is death. A dishonest person dies ultimately and untimely even.

Honesty is alias and akin to truth. Truth is singular. Lies are many and plural in number. A liar lies differently to different people as per his policy. He has to keep all lies in memories.Any disorder will invite danger and punish him severely. He always suffers from tension, lest he commits any mistake.

Truth is one and singular in number. An honest person always speaks the truth. As such an honest person has no such tension to keep all sayings in memory and track regularly lest any mishap occurs. This is why they say honesty is the best policy.

A fool wants to attain success in vain adopting dishonesty. A dishonest person realizes it when he reaches the autumn of life. At that belated period of life he cannot compensate his deficiency accumulated so far. He has nothing to do except repentance.

Policy as if is a binding. As such someone follows no policy and decide as per situation. Thus he follows instant policy which is variable in nature. Someone changes policy for gain. Someone holds policy strongly in exchange of life even.

## CONCLUSION

The authority reserves the right to take any decision which cannot be challenged. It is the policy of the administration. This is not tyranny. Rather it is autonomy. An autonomous body enjoys this power to take instant decision to avoid future complicacy. This power is exercised in the interest of public service. This policy is adopted to run the administration.

## REFERENCES

No reference, since the present article is an outcome of Creative Writing

# OF POLITICS, FEARS AND ANXIETIES

## ABSTRACT

Thus the theory goes that he who wants war does not fight but he who fights does not want war. In fact, a leader wants war but never goes to the battle field. But an unwilling soldier is compelled to go to the battle field to face gunpowder. He is charged with the sentiment to protect the chastity of motherland. But he dies and his motherland is enjoyed by the politicians. In any war or violence women and children are the worst victim.

**KEYWORDS:** Politics, fears, anxieties

## INTRODUCTION

Creative writing is based more on manifestation rather than on expression. It does not inform, rather it reveals. So it bears no reference. The best creative writing is critical, and the best critical writing is creative. This article is an outcome of thinking about creative writing meant for a general readership. As such, I have adopted a free style methodology so that everyone can enjoy the pleasure of reading. As you might know, Francis Bacon (1561-1626), the immortal essayist, wrote many essays namely 'Of Love', 'Of Friendship', 'Of Ambition', 'Of Studies', and so on. The multiple-minded genius correctly pointed out that all the words of the dictionary can be used as themes for essays But little has been done since his death to continue or finish his monumental task. Bacon's unique individual style of presentation ignited my imagination and encouraged me to write creative essays as a method of relieving a wide range of emotions through catharsis.

## ARTICLE

At present politics means polite and tricks or poly tricks. Thus, in derogatory sense, politics is the matters concerned with acquiring or exercising power within a group or an organization. As such intelligent people accept politics as profession. In politics there is no permanent friend or permanent foe but only permanent interest.

Fear is an unpleasant feeling caused by the possibility of danger, pain, a threat, etc.

Sometimes somebody is afraid of somebody or something i.e., this feeling may be specific. Again it is to feel fear about doing something. A coward suffers from fear, seldom a courageous character.

Anxiety is a nervous feeling caused by fear that something bad is going to happen. Also a strong wish for something or to do something means anxiety. Mother always suffers from anxiety lest her children face danger. Constant anxiety causes disease and affects the psyche. So, one must find out the root of anxiety and try to remove it and thereby get relief.

Horror is a feeling of intense fear, shock, dislike, hatred or disgust. It is the extremely unpleasant nature of something. A tender mind cannot bear the shocks caused by horror which affects it psychologically. But a hardened soul enjoys the film designed to entertain people like them by causing enjoyable feelings of horror. A child who behaves very badly is a little horror.

Fear, when reaches its extreme level, gives birth to terror. Thus, terror is the alias of extreme fear or horror. It is so violent that it sterilizes stamina of the victim. There are three types of terror viz., constructive terror, destructive terror and constant terror. A teacher is the terror to an inattentive student. But teacher constructs the career of a student. So, it is constructive terror. A war is a destructive horror. A dacoit falls within the same category.

In some disturbed society or in case of civil war there is always social unrest. It is the example of constant terror. People either become accustomed to it or sometimes constant terror causes mental disorder of the mass as a whole.

A pious heart believes that God created men. Conversely, one school of thought argues that men created God. To them God is merely a hypothesis. Everybody is afraid of God for His immense power. Thus, God is manmade unconquerable terror.

Death is the greatest weapon of God. God grants immortality to none. So, everybody respects and surrenders to God for peace and happiness. This surrender originates from death phobia. Thus, through death God rules over the creation and enjoys surrendering of devotee. But a pious soul has conquered death. To him death is the alias of life. To him life and death have no difference at all, on the contrary, both are equal and at par and these two are merely staying in two different places. So, he is not afraid of death but he is afraid of God lest God does not grant him shelter to His lap for eternal peace. Thus death is a terror to a common man, but seldom to a saint.

They say a terror has no substitute. A terror itself is its substitute. Thus a terror can be defended by another terror. But this doctrine is destructive. Because, it will increase terror ceaselessly and the world will be infested with terrorist as is experienced today.

Terror is bad both for body and mind. So, one should remove it from the root. Never should it be replaced by another terror. If it is allowed to persist it increases abruptly. As such to get relief from terror a student must read attentively. Similarly, war and dacoit should be faced boldly or image should be so created that opposite party must avoid war or come to a treaty and dacoit must not come for being caught red handed instead.

Likewise, to get rid of constant terror constant fight is required. In fact a man faces ceaseless terror till death. As such a man must be mentally prepared to face it. A coward always suffers from phobia. But to a brave muscle a terror is not a terror at all until or unless a terror terrorizes him.

Imperialism is the cause of war. Again, violence turns into war when two rival nations quarrel with each other. The horror of war is beggars description. The soldiers hail from poor family. A poor man dies unfed and unknown. Similarly, a soldier dies unpaid, unfed, unwept, unsung and unknown as well. As such common people seldom welcome war.

Thus the theory goes that he who wants war does not fight but he who fights does not want war. In fact, a leader wants war but never goes to the battle field. But an unwilling soldier is compelled to go to the battle field to face gunpowder. He is charged with the sentiment to protect the chastity of motherland. But he dies and his motherland is enjoyed by the politicians. In any war or violence women and children are the worst victim.

A political leader is always shrewd. But a brute can't be a leader. Shrewd orders, brute carries out. In fact a shrewd leader uses brain and a brute cadre uses hand. So, in case of any illegal event, like murder investigation reveals that the brain and hand belong to two different persons. A lay man is bound to work hard for livelihood. But a shrewd character hardly works hard. He always makes one work. That's why, he who works on behalf of a leader is called right hand. Thus brain of shrewd and body of brute make a complete man. Now, when both brutality and shrewdness are mingled in any character then it becomes dangerously brilliant or brilliantly dangerous or both simultaneously.

## CONCLUSION

Politicians welcome riots for their gain. Mob fights on behalf of the leader. They fight for the sake of fight. They fight aimlessly against each other and die. A leader seldom dies. He is the cause of death but never dies. History is the witness of many massacres.

## REFERENCES

No reference, since the present article is an outcome of Creative Writing

# *OF PROVOCATION*

## ABSTRACT

In every riot or massacre there is provocation of the protagonist. In case of communal riot it becomes violent. A fool can easily be provoked, seldom a wise. A wise seldom steps in that trap. The learned seldom provokes and never be provoked. It is the tool of a sly person. In politics it is the worst tool used against the opponent.

**KEYWORDS:**Provoke, angry, annoy, irritate, instigate, tempt, allure.

## INTRODUCTION

Creative writing is based more on manifestation rather than on expression. It does not inform, rather it reveals. So it bears no reference. The best creative writing is critical, and the best critical writing is creative. This article is an outcome of thinking about creative writing meant for a general readership. As such, I have adopted a free style methodology so that everyone can enjoy the pleasure of reading. As you might know, Francis Bacon (1561-1626), the immortal essayist, wrote many essays namely 'Of Love', 'Of Friendship', 'Of Ambition', 'Of Studies', and so on. The multiple-minded genius correctly pointed out that all the words of the dictionary can be used as themes for essays. But little has been done since his death to continue or finish his monumental task. Bacon's unique individual style of presentation ignited my imagination and encouraged me to write creative essays as a method of relieving a wide range of emotions through catharsis.

## ARTICLE

Provoke is to make a person or an animal angry or annoyed. It is the action of making somebody angry by deliberately doing something annoying or offensive. It is to cause a particular reaction in somebody.

Provoke is to rouse or incite e.g. provoked him to fury. It is to annoy, irritate. It is to call forth. It is to instigate indignation, an inquiry, a storm, etc. It is to irritate or stimulate a person. It is to tempt. It is to allure. It is to cause, give rise to e.g. will provoke fermentation.

Provoke is to anger, exasperate, or vex. It is to stir up, arouse, or call forth feelings, desires, or activity. It is to incite or stimulate to action. It is to induce or bring about. It is to summon, now obsolete.

Provoke is to excite to some action or feeling. It is to anger, irritate, or annoy. It is to evoke e.g. to provoke a laughter/riots/smiles/violence.It is to call out, challenge now obsolete. It is to excite with anger or sexual desire.

Provocative is tending, or designed, to provoke or excite anything that provokes. It is a thing tending to cause provocation of curiosity, anger, lust, etc. It is provoking or tending to provoke, as to action, thought, feeling, etc. It is stimulating, erotic, irritating, etc.

Provocative is tending to provoke, especially, anger or sexual desire. It is intentionally annoying e.g. a provocative thing; a provocative comment/remark/speech. It is intended to make somebody sexually excited or interested e.g.make a provocative gesture. She was dressed to look provocative.

Provocation is the act or an instance of provoking. It is a state of being provoked e.g. did it under severe provocation. It is a cause of annoyance. Legally, it is an action, insult, etc. held to be likely to provoke physical retaliation.

Provocation is something that provokes. It is, especially, a cause of resentment or irritation. It is any cause of danger. It is something that incites, instigates, angers, or irritatese.g. downs tools at or on the slightest provocation.

Provoking is that provokes, especially, annoying or vexing.

Provoke somebody into doing something/to do something is to make somebody do something by continually annoying them or treating them in a certain way.

Provoker is one to evoke. It reminds past days. It causes to enjoy nostalgia.

Provocateur is one who provokes unrest and dissatisfaction for political ends.

Provoke, excite, stimulate, pique are synonymous.

Provoke implies rather generally an arousing to some action or feeling e.g. thought provoking. Excite suggests a more powerful or profound stirring or moving of the thoughts or emotions e.g. it excites my imagination. Stimulate implies an arousing as if by goading or pricking and, hence, often connotes a bringing out of a state of inactivity or indifference e.g. to stimulate one's enthusiasm. Pique suggests a stimulating as if by irritating mildly e.g. to pique one's curiosity.

Annoy, aggravate, infuriate, irritate are synonyms of provoke.

Calm and propitiate are antonyms of provoke.

Provocation is a nasty game. It is derogatory in nature. It is the tool of idle brains for gaining profit.  It is the dirty business of the dirty people. It discloses true identity of the shrewd person thus involved.

Man provokes. He has to provoke. He is bound to provoke. Similarly, man is provoked. He is bound to be provoked. In this regard he is quite undone except experiencing self-provocation quite helplessly. Thus man willy-nilly faces provocations infinite times from cradle to coffin in its various forms and features having different degrees and dimensions along with various faces and facets as well.

I am not easily provoked, but his behavior is intolerable. If you provoke the dog, it will attack you. His selfish behavior finally provoked her into leaving him. He was provoked by their repeated questioning to say more than he had intended. He reacted with violence only under provocation i.e. when provoked. She loses her temper at/on the slightest provocation. The police remained calm in the face of repeated provocations. Ignore him – he is just being provocative.His speech provoked an angry reaction/response from the crowd. It is very provoking of her to be so late.In assaulting him he had acted under severe provocation. The abuses were enough provocation for the reprisal. She looked provocative in that mini-skirt. Even tame buffaloes can be dangerous when provoked. Her insulting remarks provoked me to dismiss her. The comment provoked a roar of laughter. The new legislation nearly provoked a riot.

Man becomes the prey of provocation for gaining profit. Instant profit allures him to provoke or to be provoked. Greed is alias and akin to sin. The wage of sin is death. A fool dies being driven by greed. As such they say look before you leap. If the profit is by way of honest means there lays no risk or problem.

There are two types of persons. The first category avoids provocation. The second category invites provocation for personal gain. It is his business. In provoked situation everybody remains tensed. But the shrewd person remains calm and performs his operation silently and successfully. He is so genius. He is such a finished scoundrel who seldom does any mistake.

In every riot or massacre there is provocation of the protagonist. In case of communal riot it becomes violent. A fool can easily be provoked, seldom a wise. A wise seldom steps in that trap. The learned seldom provokes and never be provoked. It is the tool of a sly person. In politics it is the worst tool used against the opponent.

Man sometimes protests against provocation. Sometimes he remains aloof. Thus his mood and motif are gloriously so uncertain. This assumption is not correct at all. Whatever man does, he does to serve and satisfy his own interest only. This unique formula of man's nature and behaviour can explain of any action or inaction uniquely. Always protest is bad, more bad not to protest at all. Man protests thereby struggles for existence.

Provocative dress invites sexual harassment. It is quite debatable. A person may be provoked by any event. Identical event may not create any sensation equally or create no pulse at all to another one. It depends on taste and temperament of the concerned person. It depends more on the culture as well. What is accepted or quite normal in a culture is totally banned in another culture due to orthodoxy. Culture offers didactic lessons to its followers. Its essence is based on moral values. It teaches etiquette.


## CONCLUSION

Thought provoking is quite different from normal provocation that causes anger or annoyance or both simultaneously. It ignites imagination already in man. It gives birth to many theories or invention. It is positive in nature. It is optimist. It implies inquisitiveness. It is curiosity. It paves the avenue of advancement of civilization.

## REFERENCES

No reference, since the present article is an outcome of Creative Writing

.